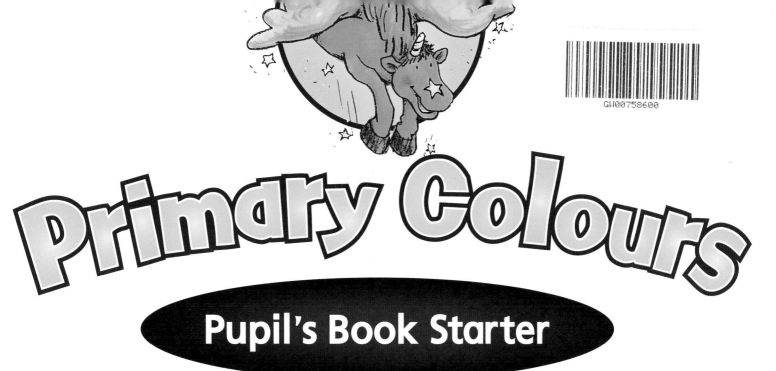

Primary Colours

Pupil's Book Starter

Diana Hicks   **Andrew Littlejohn**

CAMBRIDGE
UNIVERSITY PRESS

CAMBRIDGE UNIVERSITY PRESS
Cambridge, New York, Melbourne, Madrid, Cape Town,
Singapore, São Paulo, Delhi, Mexico City

Cambridge University Press
The Edinburgh Building, Cambridge CB2 8RU, UK

www.cambridge.org
Information on this title: www.cambridge.org/9780521667357

First published 2002
12th printing 2013

Printed and bound in the United Kingdom by the MPG Books Group

A catalogue record for this publication is available from the British Library

ISBN 978-0-521-66735-7 Pupil's Book
ISBN 978-0-521-66731-9 Activity Book
ISBN 978-0-521-66727-2 Teacher's Book
ISBN 978-0-521-75096-7 Class Audio CDs (2)
ISBN 978-0-521-66723-4 Class Audio Cassettes (2)
ISBN 978-0-521-75097-4 Songs and Stories Audio CD
ISBN 978-0-521-66719-7 Songs and Stories Cassette
ISBN 978-0-521-66715-9 Vocabulary Cards

Contents

1 Me and you

1A Hello!

1 🔊 Listen.

2 🔊 Listen and point.

3 🔊 Sing a song.

1B Hello, Nico!

1 🎵 Listen and point.

2 🎚️ Listen and point.

1

2

3

4

3 🎚️ Sing a song.

1C Goodbye!

1 🔊 Listen and say.

2 📻 Look, say and listen.

1

2

3

4

3 Play a game.

1D Nico and I can make ...

1 🔊 Listen and point.

2 Play a game.

③ Make finger puppets.

You need:

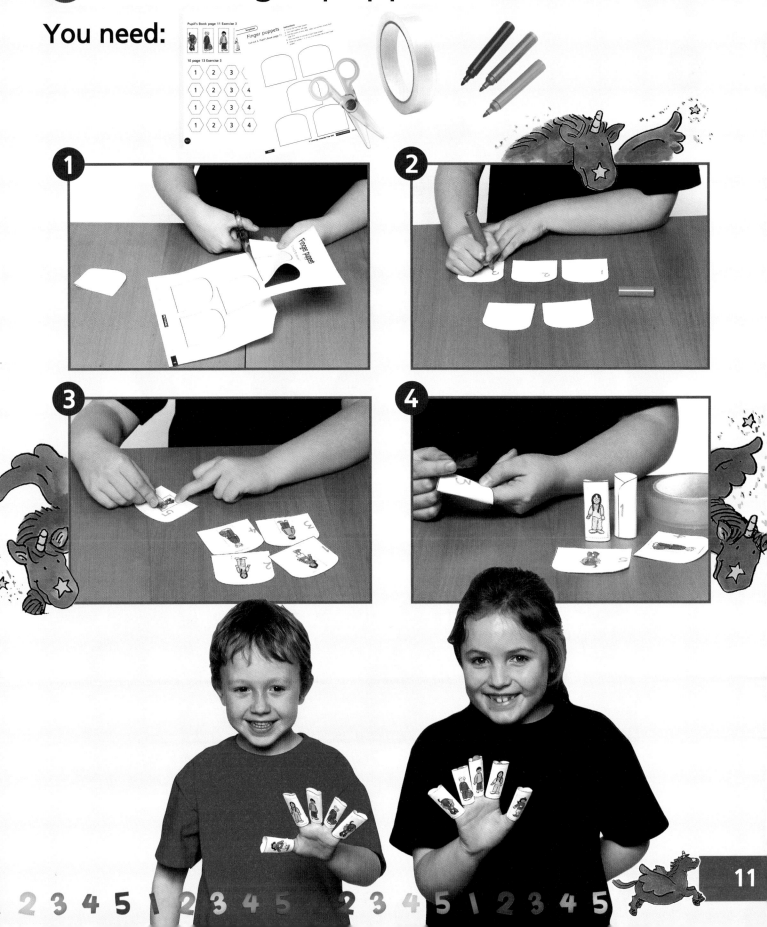

1 Say *Hello* and *Goodbye*.

2 Look and say.

3 Play a game.

4  Sing a song.

2 My school

2A In my bag

1  Listen and look.

2 🎵 Listen, point and say.

1

2

3

4

5

3 🎵 Sing a song.

2B In my classroom

1  Say a chant.

2 Look, point and say.

In our classroom

3 Listen and point. Listen and match.

2C Nico in the classroom

1 🔊 Listen and look.

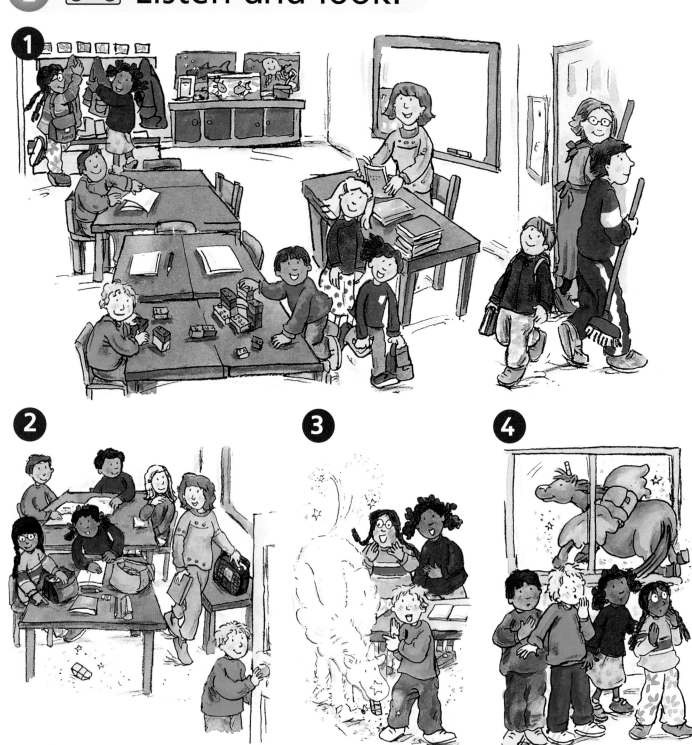

2 Say and do.

1

2

3

3 🎵 Sing a song.

19

2D Nico and I can make ...

1 🔊 Listen, point and say.

2 🔊 Look and count. Listen and check.

① **②** **③** **④** **⑤**

③ Make a birthday card.

You need:

2E I can say ...

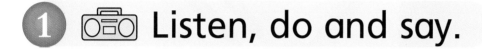

1 Listen, do and say.

1

2

3

4

22

2 Look, point and say.

1

2

3

4

5

6

3 🎵 Sing a song.

3 Playtime

3A I can play!

1 🔊 Listen, look and say.

2 🔊 Look and match.
Listen, check and say.

Bella   Eddie   Anna   Lee   Nico

3 🔊 Sing a song.

1 🔊 Look and listen.

1

2

2 🔊 Look and say. Listen and check.

1

2

3 Play a game.

3C Can you swim?

1 📻 **Look and listen.**

2 Look and ask.

1 **2** **3** **4**

5 **6** **7** **8**

3 🔊 Sing a song.

3D Nico and I can make ...

1 Listen and point.

2 Look and match. Listen and check.

Aa Anna

Bb bike

Cc cake

Ff

Ll

Mm

Nn

book

Mrs Martin

Lee

felt tip

football

Nico

bag

3 Make an alphabet book.

You need:

3E I can say ...

1 🔊 Listen, look and write.

1

2

3

4

5

6

7

8

9

10

2 Look and ask.

1 ☐

2 ☐

3 ☐

4 ☐

5 ☐

6 ☐

7 ☐

8 ☐

3 🔊 Sing a song.

4 At home

4A   We can fly!

1 🎙️ Look and listen.

34

2 📻 Listen, look and write.

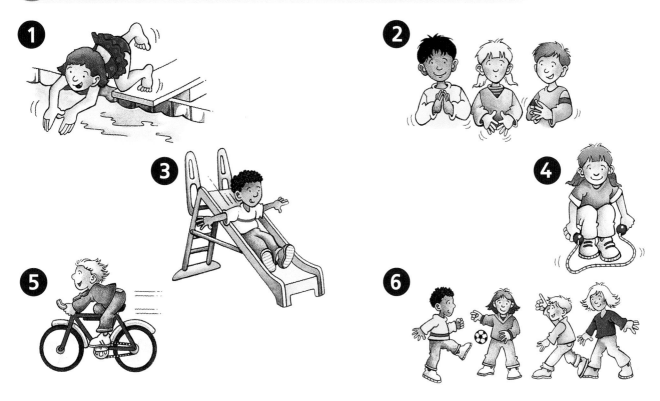

1

2

3

4

5

6

3 Look, think and say.

4B How many?

1 Choose, count and say.

1

2

2 🔊 Listen and write.

	a	**b**	**c**	**d**	**e**	**f**	**g**	**h**
Bella	1							
Eddie								

3 🔊 Sing a song.

4C Nico can help!

1 Look and listen.

1a

1b Help!

2 Where's Lee?

3

4 Where's Lee?

5 Where's Anna?

6

2 Look, think and say.

1
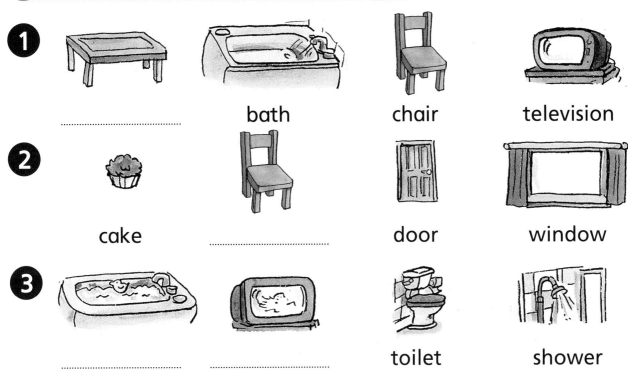

....   bath   chair   television

2
cake   ....   door   window

3
....   toilet   shower

3 Listen and match.

Bella

Eddie

Anna

Lee

39

4D Nico and I can make ...

1 🎛 Listen and point.

2 🎛 Say a chant.

3 🎛 Listen, look and match.

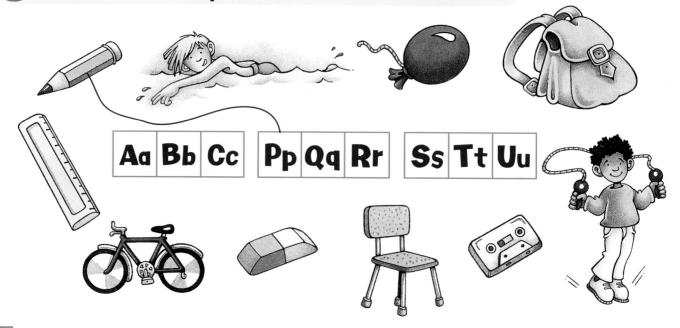

Aa Bb Cc | Pp Qq Rr | Ss Tt Uu

Aa Bb Cc Dd Ee Ff Gg Hh Ii Jj K

4 Make alphabet pockets.

You need:

1 ## Look, match and say.

he   she   we

2 🎙️ ## Play a game.

3 Look, choose and say.

a

b

c

d

e

1 kitchen

2 bedroom

3 bathroom

4 living room

f

g

h

i

5 Things I like

1 Look and listen.

1 I like yellow.

2 I like blue.

3 I like red.

4 I like green.

5

2 🔊 Listen and match.

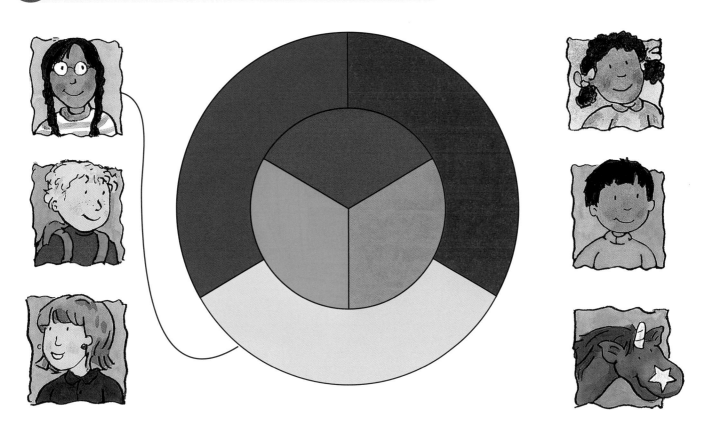

3 🔊 Sing a song.

45

5B Magic fingers!

1 📻 Look, listen and find.

You can paint with your fingers.

You can paint with your hands.

You can't paint with your feet!

Eddie

2 Look, choose, draw and say.

1

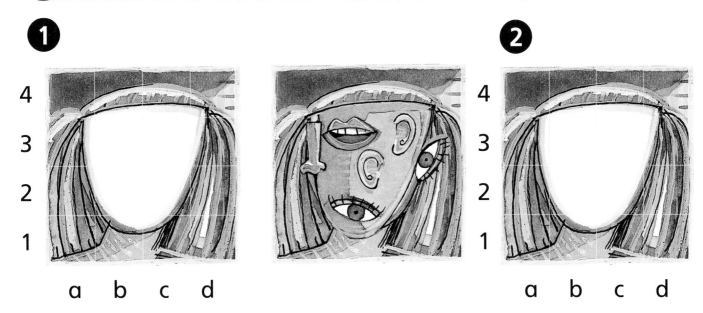

4
3
2
1

a   b   c   d

2

4
3
2
1

a   b   c   d

3 Match, listen and say.

5C My body

1 🔊 Listen, look and find.

1

2

3

4

5

2 🎙 Count, listen and match.

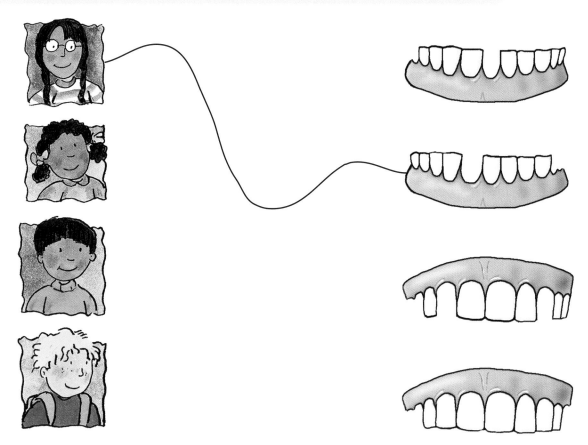

3 🎙 Sing a song.

5D Nico and I can make ...

1 🎙 Write, listen and match.

1   r ....

2

3   ...green...

     y ....

4   y .... r .... b .... g ....

5   b ....

2 🎙 Sing a song.

3 Make a toothbrush chart.

You need:

5E I can say …

1 📻 Listen and play.

①

a		c
i		k
v		x

②

b	h	
j	p	
r		t

③

d		f
l		n
q		s

④

e		g
m		o
u		w

2 📻 Sing a song.

3 🔊 Listen and write.

	Lee	Anna	Eddie	Bella
I can ...	1, 5			
I can't ...				
I've got ...	a			

4 Look and say.

6 Holidays!

6A Rainbow days!

1 🎙️ Listen and find.

Tuesday   Monday   Friday   Thursday   Wednesday

2 Look and say.

is   are

3 🎙️ Sing a song.

6B Nico's purple weekend!

1   Look, listen and point.

Nico is happy. Nico likes purple.

2 Listen and write.

a [1]   b [ ]   c [ ]

d [ ]   e [ ]   f [ ]

6C Dressing-up is fun!

1 Listen and look.

2 Look, think and say.

hat   sweater   coat

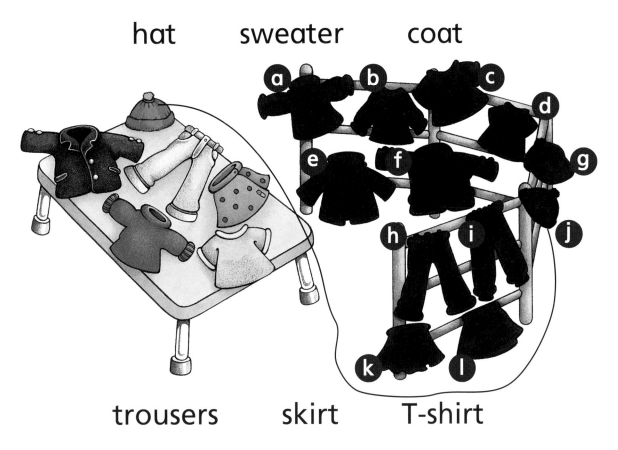

trousers   skirt   T-shirt

3 🎵 Sing a song.

6D Nico and I can make ...

1 🎵 Sing a song.

2 🎵 Listen and match.

Bella

Eddie

we | in

The happy weekend

magic

in

Lee

Anna

③ Make a Nico bookmark.

You need:

I can say...

1 Play a game.

Thanks and Acknowledgements

Dedication

Diana would like to dedicate Primary Colours to all children around the world whose lives still lack basic human rights. Andrew thanks the many children who have shown him how we continually underestimate how much children really can do, given the chance.

Authors' thanks

Grateful thanks to Sue Ullstein at Cambridge University Press for her delicate editorial control and to Maria Pylas for managing, seemingly tirelessly, to fit the innumerable pieces of the course's jigsaw into a coherent whole. Thanks also are due to Ruth Atkinson for transforming a complex Teacher's Book typescript into a readable book. Our thanks also go to the design team at Pentacor and all the artists who have so colourfully transformed our verbal world into a visual one, and the Cambridge offices around the world who have helped us tailor the materials to the needs of the teachers they serve.

Special congratulations are very much due to Robert Lee and Tim Wharton for making wonderful music from our lyrics.

The authors and publishers would like to thank the following teachers and institutions for their help in testing the material and for the invaluable feedback which they provided:

Norma Cristina Cardarelli, Escuela No. 14, Martínez, Marta Ferrari, Escuela Cristóforo Colombo, Ramsay, Karina Pereiro Miñan, Escuela No. 11 1057 Brandsen, Buenos Aires, Argentina; Ana Maria Alvarez, Escuela No. 11 1057 Brandsen, Buenos Aires, Veronica Jordan Lopez, Instituto Summa Yerbal, Buenos Aires, Argentina; Vlastislava Vilcáková, Základní škola, Prague, Libuse Drkulová, Základní škola, Prague, Czech Republic; Sanaa Naguib Zaki, Sahara Language School, Cairo, Egypt; Anne Thimonier-Mathieu, Ecole Les Páquerettes, Nanterre, Colette Samson, IUFM de Versailles, Versailles, France; Vasso Ganou-Stefa, Vasso Ganou-Stefa, Nikea, Stamatina Kamuissi, Ganou Language Centre, Nikea, Irene Savvas, Geitonas School, Vari, Katerina Kassimati, Geitonas School, Vari, Ioanna Anagnostopoulou, Geitonas School, Vari, Maria Sotirchou, Geitonas School, Vari, Kelly Mandalou, Geitonas School, Vari, Effie Assimou, Geitonas School, Vari, Maria Antonopoulou, Geitonas School, Attikis, Katerina Pappas, Geitonas School, Vari, Paraskevi Kanastra, Gavatha Language School, Athens, Maria Haragioni, Gavatha Language School, Halandri, Virginia Gavatha, Gavatha Language School, Halandri, Penny Jemis, Doukas School, Marousi, Maria Stamatoudi, Costeas-Geitonas School, Pallini-Attikis, Adrian Bezouglof, Adrian Bezouglof Language School, Perama, Marika Missirli, Costeas-Geitonas School, Pallini-Attikis, Valerie Turner, Costeas-Geitonas School, Pallini-Attikis, Leda Bandavas, Costeas-Gitonas School, Pallini-Attikis, Rania Giovanopoulou, Doukas School, Marousi, Ann Bassel Vassilaki, Doukas School, Marousi, Marie Xenou, Doukas School, Marousi, Annette Morley, Doukas School, Marousi, Greece; Havelda Miklósné, Általános Iskola, Budaörs, Poór Zsuzsánna, Rainbow English Language Activity School, Veszprém, Hungary; Gabriella Cuman Giometto, Scuola Elementare Statale "G.G. Trissino", Vicenza, Lucarini Paola, Primary School Zambelli, Falconara, Biancoli Roberta, Scuola Elementare "G. Zanardi", Bologna, Biancoli Roberta, Scuola Elementare "G. Zanardi", Bologna, Simonetta Nasoni, Scuola Elementare Statale "Bambini Di Sarajevo", Bologna, Italy; Adriana Urritia Orozco, Instituto Anglo Americano, Mexico City, Mexico; Margarita Montoya, Magister School, Lima, Patricia Alarco, Magister School, Lima, Peru; Justyna Piechowiak, Szkoła Języków Obcych, Gniezno, Magdalena Krzyżanowska, Kursy Języka Angielskiego Firma "Yes", Warsaw, Ewa Markiewicz, XVI Społeczna Szkoła Podstawowa, Warsaw, Poland; Nina Gorghanova, St Petersburg, Irene Sventsitsky, Russian Gymnasium 1567, Kutuzovski proyezd, Russia; Cilka Demšar, Evropa d.o.o. Bled, Bled, Lidija Perko, Little England Club Language School, Kamnik, Gaborovič Barbara, Little England Club Language School, Kamnik, Tjaša Milijaš, OŠ Dravlje, Ljubljana, Vera Boštjančič-Turk, Yezikovni Center, Ljubljana, Natasa Halnar, Yurena, Novo Mesto, Mihaela Brkopec, Yurena, Novo Mesto, Katja Hrovat, Yurena, Novo Mesto, Mateja Tramte, Yurena, Novo Mesto, Nada Gruden, Pionirski DOM-CKM, Ljubljana, Slovenia; Isabel Busquets Corbera, Escola Del Mar, Barcelona, Sílvia Pardàs, C.E.I.P Les Clisques, Port De La Selva, Joana Ferragut Bonet, C.E.I.P.M. Barkeno, Barcelona, Caroline Davies, C.P. Cervantes, Madrid, Nicolás Serna, C.P. Francisco de Quevedo, Madrid, Josefina Inclán Nichol, C.P. Cervantes, Madrid, Alicia Vico Román, C.P. Julio Verne, Madrid, José Javier Martínez de Imes, C.P. Cervantes, Madrid, Berta Nieto, C.P. Julio Verne, Madrid, José B. Torres Díaz, Colegio "Lazarillo de Tormes", Madrid, Susana Calderón Toro, New Center International College, Madrid, Spain; Kathleen Shirley Aytaç, Özel Mimar Sinan Lisesi, Istanbul, Ibrahim Metin Özlü, Özel Akdenis Lisesi, Adana, Deb Molster, Özel Acarlar Koleji, Istanbul, Turkey.

The authors and publishers would like to thank the following teachers for their help in reviewing the material and for the invaluable feedback which they provided:

Silvia Ronchetti, Clover English Language Centre, Buenos Aires, Argentina; Maria Heloisa Alves Audino, Colégio Nossa Senhora de Sion-Vila Maria, São Paulo, Brazil; Margareth Perucci, Cultura Inglesa, São Paulo, Brazil; Rosario Infante, Colegios Padre Hurtado y Juanita de Los Andes, Santiago, Chile; Nadia Vojtková, Gymnázium Slapanice, Slapanice, Czech Republic; Maha Seifein Ebeid, El. Nasr Schools Heliopolis, Cairo, Egypt; Claire Dorey, Institut de la Providence, Paris, Annie Brun, IUFM de Lorraine, Epinal, France; Catherine Johnson-Stefanidou, Johnson-Stefanidou School of Foreign Languages, Thessaloniki, Elsa Plakida, Arsakeio School, Thessaloniki, Christine Barton, Patras, Katerina Stavridou, Svarna Schools of English, Thessaloniki, Greece; Zsófia Tettamanti, Bell Schools, Budapest, Hungary; Fabiola Isidori, San Lazzaro, Italy; Oliver Page, Perugia, Italy; Olga Pretelini, Martha Cedeño, Colegio Cristobal Colón, Edo. de México, Mexico; Magdalena Kijak, Szkoła Jezyków Obcych EMPIK, Krakow, Ewa Markiewicz, XVI Społeczna Szkoła Podstawowa, Warsaw, Elźbieta Kopocz, Elkop-Translations Language School, Katowice, Poland; Julya Ryapolova, Moscow, Russia; Elena Borisovna Polyakova, Edučational Centre "Gazprom" Primary School, Moscow, Russia; Jezerka Beskovnik, OS Lucija, Portoros, Slovenia; Maria Teresa Díaz, C.P. Aldebarain, Madrid, Spain; Mercedes de la Ossa, Spain; Carmen Vidal Medigldea, Madrid, Spain; Tülay Erpolat, Özel Çakabey Koleji, Izmir, Celia Gasgil, Özel Izmir Türk Koleji, Izmir, Turkey; Vivi Delevi, Özel İstanbul Koleji, Istanbul, Carolyn Güven, Özel Sezin Okullari, Istanbul, Turkey; Taisa Varskaya, Secondary School 175, Kiev, Galina Kashko, Specialised Language School 135, Kiev, Ukraine; Gill Budgell, Consultant, Cambridge, Susan Hughes, Consultant, Cambridge, UK.

The authors and publishers are grateful to the following illustrators:

Sami Sweeten, c/o Heather Richards Agency; Susan Hutchison; Amelia Rosata, c/o Heather Richards Agency; Lisa Smith, c/o Sylvie Poggio Artists.

The authors and publishers would like to thank the children at St Matthews Primary School, Cambridge, for participating so enthusiastically while being photographed and David Someville, the headmaster, for allowing us into the school.

Commissioned photos by Gareth Boden Photography.

Cover design by Pentacor Book Design.

Cover illustration by David Shenton.

Book design and page make-up by Pentacor Book Design.

Sound recordings by Anne Rosenfeld, RBA productions, at Studio AVP.

Song words By Diana Hicks and Andrew Littlejohn.

Music by Robert Lee and Tim Wharton.